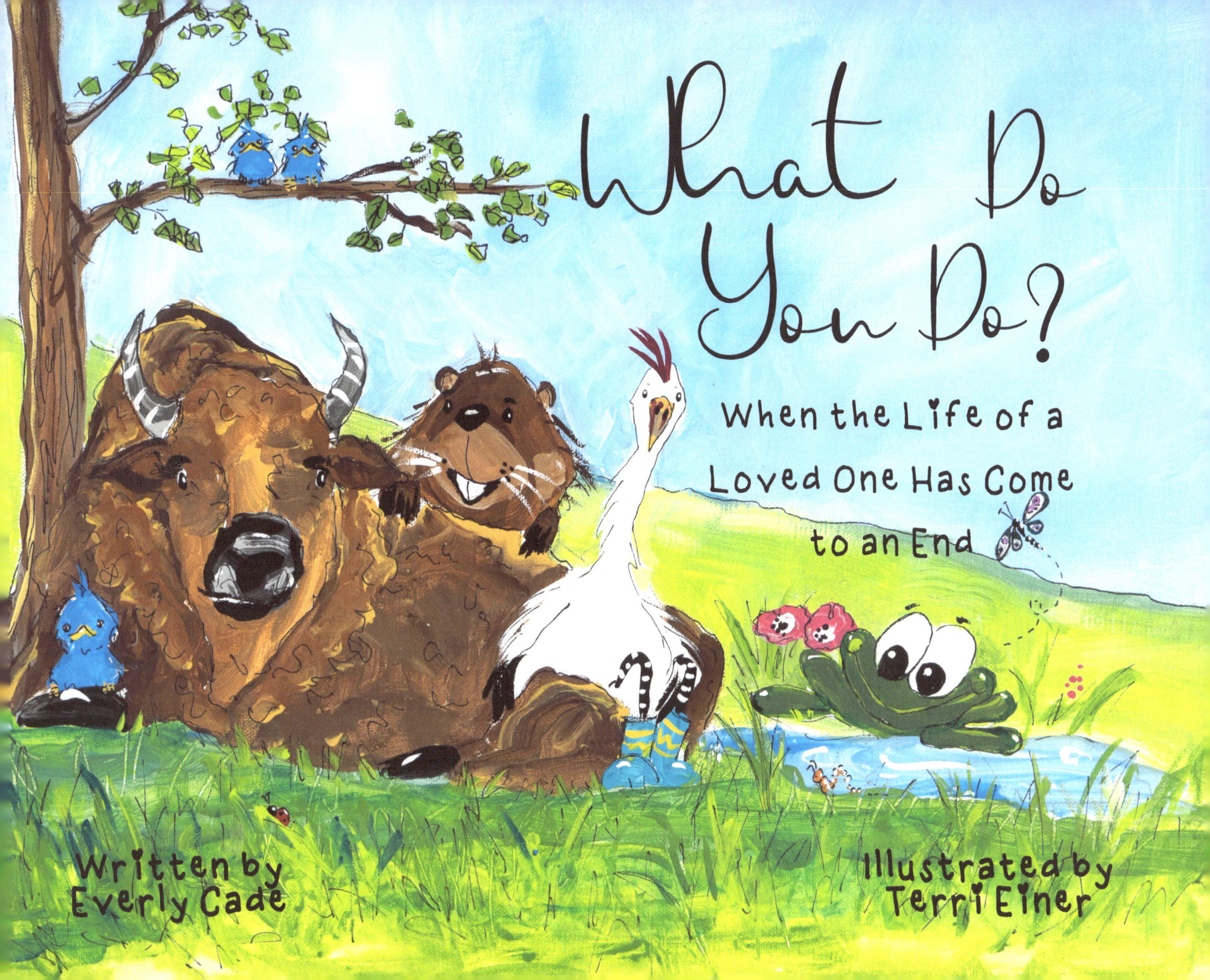

This book is dedicated to YOU.

"It's the beauty within us that makes it possible for us to recognize the beauty around us.

The question is not what you look at but what you see."
Henry David Thoreau

I wish you to see all the beauty!

You came into this world on a bright, starry night.

Then, you left much too quickly, and gone was your light.

Every day, Mom and Dad were so quiet and sad,
and I felt so alone. Yes, at times, even mad.

Something terrible happened; my brother was gone
from our life here, today, and the future beyond.

I felt lost with how crazy and awful things were,
as day-in and day-out, it just all seemed to blur.

When my parents were ready to talk, they would start
simply sharing their pain—and the hole in their heart.

I would tell them, "I'm missing my brother—like you.

I feel lost and alone. I don't know what to do."

"I will miss him forever,
but I am still here.

Don't forget about me
when I need you so near."

Then, Mom gathered me close
as she snuggled me tight.

And we promised we'd talk
'til we're nearly alright.

She explained, "It's okay that we're feeling so sad."

"I'll make sure that you won't feel alone," she would add.

Then we talked about Archie as if he were here,
sharing all we remembered—our tears and his cheer.

Though he might not be here, he brought light to our lives.
Our affection for him and each other survives.

I'm afraid I'll forget him, but what can I do?
What could help me recall? How do others pull through?

I will go take a walk, asking friends how they mend when the life of a loved one has come to an end.

First, I met Mr. Frog in his pond near the sod.
And I asked how he copes —since his wife is with God.

Well, he thought for a minute, and then he replied,
"I plant flowers right here at my home, with great pride."

"As I water these flowers with all of my love,
I am sure that she watches and smiles from above."

So, I wrote down his answer, and then, right on-track,
came a Bison who carried three birds on her back.

"Mrs. Bison," I asked, "Tell me how you go on and continue with life when your loved ones are gone."

Well, she thought for a minute, and then she replied, "Quite a few things have helped me whenever I've tried."

"First, I speak of them often—and talk to them too,
'cause our love for each other will carry me through."

"Then, I hug myself hard, and it feels like it's them.
If you give it a try, you will feel like a gem."

Shortly, one of the birds wisely opened her beak .
She had something to say, and she needed to speak.

She proceeded to chirp in a comforting tone :
"I can carry their toy or their favorite stone."

"I tell no one about it; not one creature sees.
But it's there in my pocket and puts me at ease."

So, I wrote down her answer, and then I moved on.
Next, I came to a Dragonfly: Mr. LeBron.

I remarked, "I'm afraid
to be one who forgets.
What is getting you through?
Do you have some regrets?"

Very promptly, he answered,
"You'll never forget!
They remain in your heart
from the moment you met."

"You'll remember their smile
and their laughter so good—
about things that you shared
on this Earth when you could."

"From the moment my loved one departed from here,
I could still feel their love, and I know they are near."

"They are here when I'm happy. And still, when I'm sad,
I can feel their bright spirit, which makes me feel glad."

So, I wrote down his answer,
and then I moved on
to a wonderful friend
that I happened upon.

To this friend, Mrs. Beaver,
I mentioned my fears
that I'd soon forget Archie
and all of my tears.

So, I asked, "Mrs. Beaver,
say, what do you do
to hold onto your loved ones,
whose life, here, is through?"

First, she thought for a minute,
and then she replied,
"We could never forget them—
No, not if we tried!"

"Our unstoppable feelings
for loved ones will flow.
So, we plant baby trees,
and we watch how they grow."

As I wrote down her answer, I knew I was done.
All the answers I'd heard had been great. Every one!

I'd been walking all day, and I saw the sun set.
I'd be heading for home, so my parents won't fret.

It had been a long day when my Mom tucked me in.

When we snuggled, she asked if my day was a win.

I recalled all the things my friends told me they did:
Planting flowers and trees; trinkets carried and hid.

"Well, I learned a great thing: There's no way I'll forget.
Little Archie's been part of me since we first met!"